Saint Joan of Arc

Saint Joan of Arc

God's Soldier

Written by
Susan Helen Wallace, FSP

Illustrated by
Ray Morelli

Pauline
BOOKS & MEDIA

Boston

Library of Congress Cataloging-in-Publication Data

Wallace, Susan Helen, 1940–

   Saint Joan of Arc, God's soldier / written by Susan Helen Wallace, ; illustrated by Ray Morelli.

     p. cm. — (Encounter the saints series ; 7)

Summary: A biography of the fifteenth-century peasant girl who led French armies at God's command, was burned at the stake as a heretic, and later canonized a saint by the Roman Catholic Church. Includes a prayer and glossary of terms.

   ISBN 0-8198-7033-1 (pbk.)

   1. Joan, of Arc, Saint, 1412–1431—Juvenile literature. 2. Christian women saints—France—Biography— Juvenile literature. [1. Joan, of Arc, Saint, 1412–1431. 2. Saints. 3. Women—Biography.]   I. Morelli, Ray, ill. II. Title. III. Series.

   DC103.5 .W35 2000

   944'.026'092—dc21

                                                        00-008422

"P" and PAULINE are registered trademarks of the Daughters of St. Paul

Copyright © 2000, Daughters of St. Paul

Published in the U.S.A. by Pauline Books & Media, 50 Saint Pauls Avenue, Boston, MA 02130-3491.

Printed in U.S.A

www.pauline.org

Pauline Books & Media is the publishing house of the Daughters of St. Paul, an international congregation of women religious serving the Church with the communications media.

3 4 5 6 7 8   10 09 08 07 06 05

Encounter the Saints Series

Blesseds Jacinta and Francisco Marto
Shepherds of Fatima

Blessed Pier Giorgio Frassati
Journey to the Summit

Blessed Teresa of Calcutta
Missionary of Charity

Journeys with Mary
Apparitions of Our Lady

Saint Anthony of Padua
Fire and Light

Saint Bernadette Soubirous
Light in the Grotto

Saint Edith Stein
Blessed by the Cross

Saint Elizabeth Ann Seton
Daughter of America

Saint Frances Cabrini
Cecchina's Dream

Saint Francis of Assisi
Gentle Revolutionary

Saint Ignatius of Loyola
For the Greater Glory of God

Saint Isaac Jogues
With Burning Heart

Saint Joan of Arc
God's Soldier

Saint Juan Diego
And Our Lady of Guadalupe

Saint Julie Billiart
The Smiling Saint

Saint Katharine Drexel
The Total Gift

Saint Martin de Porres
Humble Healer

Saint Maximilian Kolbe
Mary's Knight

Saint Pio of Pietrelcina
Rich in Love

Saint Thérèse of Lisieux
The Way of Love

For other children's titles on the Saints,
visit our Web site: www.pauline.org

CONTENTS

1

A Nightmare Comes True

"I can trust you with all the other chores, and this is no different, Joan," the gentle woman with tired eyes coaxed. "It isn't hard to light the fire. Watch me now so you can do it next time."

"No...Mother...please!" Joan begged, her own eyes brimming with tears. "I'm afraid of fire!"

"But fire is good. Look, it's already begun to cook our supper," her mother replied as she straightened up from the hearth. "We need fire—even to keep warm and healthy. Now the next time you'll get it going, won't you?"

"Maybe," Joan hesitated. "I mean, I want to try. Yes, yes, next time I'll do it!"

"You're too soft," Jacques d'Arc scolded his wife. "She weaves her way around you, Isabelle. That's no way to discipline a child."

"Now, Jacques," Mrs. d'Arc said softly. "Children have these strange fears. Be patient."

"Patient!" he shouted. "Why, Joan is thirteen years old. It's time she outgrew this foolish fear of fire. Teach her. You're her mother. Teach her!"

Life for a country girl in fifteenth-century France was hard. There were no extras. Jacques d'Arc was a peasant who had the good fortune of owning a few animals and a small piece of land that he farmed. Through careful management, Mr. d'Arc eked out a living for himself, his wife and their five children. Still, it took great effort to make ends meet, and many times he came home overtired. But Mrs. d'Arc was very wise and equally patient. She understood her husband, gruff as Jacques was. And she made sure that the children understood him, too.

All the family members had their own jobs. Joan's included housecleaning and sewing. Sometimes she also worked as a shepherdess, tending their small flock of sheep and watching over their few cows.

The family's village of Domrémy seemed ordinary enough. But fear hung over the hamlet and gnawed at the minds of everyone old enough to know how to worry.

War was a word that the villagers understood all too well. Domrémy bordered the enemy territory of Lorraine. Its tiny population could never defend itself in the event of an attack. The citizens lived in uneasy expectation.

The people knew that at any time a raid could force them to leave their homes and flee to the next town. When Burgundian bandits overran a town, they sacked, burned and destroyed everything in sight, unless the nobles of the area could pay them enough of a bribe. But would Domrémy even have anything to bargain with?

These worries preoccupied Jacques d'Arc as he stopped his work one evening. His family, his farm, his crops—years of struggle—to think it could all go up in a puff of smoke! As he wiped his damp forehead with the back of his hand, a happy voice broke in on his thoughts.

"Father! Father!" Joan called as she ran up. "Put those heavy tools away now. Supper's ready."

"Do you have to be so noisy?" Mr. d'Arc responded roughly.

"I'm sorry," Joan mumbled. "What's the matter? You look so worried."

"It's nothing," he said, ruffling her hair. "Come on. Your mother's waiting."

That same night, frantic screams split

the air. Mr. d'Arc's worst nightmare had come true.

"It's the Burgundians! The Burgundians are coming!"

Mrs. d'Arc anxiously gathered the children. "We must get up! We must go! Hurry children, quickly now!" she exclaimed. "Take your woolen capes. I hope you'll be warm enough."

"Hurry!" shouted Joan's father.

"We're ready, Jacques," her mother answered.

The family fled from the house, running as fast as possible. The night was very dark, but Mr. d'Arc knew the way. How many times he had planned this escape in his mind, knowing that his family's safety might depend on it one day.

They walked, then ran, and walked again. It was eight miles to the town of Neufchâteau. But tonight it seemed like eighty. The hours dragged on. A combination of panic and fright made Joan's legs so wobbly she could hardly walk. She imagined leaping flames devouring the village behind her, and she wanted to close her eyes and pretend it was all just a bad dream. But the frantic, pushing crowd of refugees that surrounded her wouldn't let her do that. She had to keep going.

"Will we ever go back home again?" Joan asked as hot tears slipped down her cheeks.

"Yes," her father said firmly. "Yes," he repeated, squeezing her tightly. "We'll go back—and very soon!"

The first streaks of dawn appeared as Neufchâteau came into full view. It wasn't home, but for now it meant safety and rest.

2

THE VOICE

"In the name of the Father, and of the Son, and of the Holy Spirit. Amen."

As they finished their morning prayers the next day, Joan leaned toward her mother. "Why, Mama?" she whispered. "Why is there always so much fighting?"

Mrs. d'Arc sighed. It was hard to explain what she couldn't really understand herself. But she would try....

"For many years two great European nations have been at war. The problems started when you were just a baby, Joan. At that time, King Henry V of England crossed the ocean, took over Normandy, and claimed the crown of Charles VI, our French king.

"Because Charles VI was mentally ill, his son, Charles VII, called the Dauphin, was the real king of France in most people's minds. But the Dauphin is a very unusual man," Mrs. d'Arc said, shaking her head. "As time went on, he did almost nothing to try to restore freedom to our country. Our people began to think he was a coward. And facts are facts. Outside of Charles' great gold and marble palace, where he peacefully sits enjoying dancing, games and expensive food, town after French town is falling into English hands."

Mrs. d'Arc sighed sadly as she continued, "Charles acts as though he doesn't even care. It seems he's just given up. Because he doesn't know how to cope with France's problems, he's decided to ignore them. But deep within his heart and conscience, I think the Dauphin is very troubled. He knows it's up to him to do something to save our country. He's just not brave enough to do it."

Mr. d'Arc, who had been listening silently, now broke in. "What your mother says is true. It hasn't been easy for France's powerful nobles to stay loyal to a coward. When some of the Dauphin's men went out on their own and murdered the French Duke of Burgundy, a civil war broke out. The Duke's Burgundian troops went over to the side of the English and began fighting against the Dauphin and France.

"Our poorly defended towns don't stand a chance against the well-trained English soldiers. And now with the added attacks of the Burgundians..." Mr. d'Arc's voice grew quieter, "everything really seems hopeless. Only the city of Orleans is strong enough to protect itself. But how long can the people hold out? If the English capture Orleans, it will be the end of our country."

"All we can do now is pray, Joan," Mrs. d'Arc said softly. "Only God is powerful enough to help us. But even God can't help us if we won't let him."

The d'Arc family was soon able to return home to Domrémy. The little town had never looked so beautiful to Joan. Through clever bargaining on the part of the nobles, Domrémy had been looted, but not burned. The Burgundians had left most of the peasant cottages untouched.

Joan walked slowly through the fields. She could smell the sweetness of the tall grass as a breeze caught and lifted her hair. *Creation is so beautiful,* she thought. *It reminds me of God.*

The wind gradually died down, and all was very still. Joan knelt in a small clearing. She gathered her thoughts and began to pray. She often talked to God like this—very simply, as her Friend. Afterward she always felt better, and she found it easier to do her chores around the house.

In the stillness Joan suddenly heard a deep voice. "Joan...Joan of Arc," it called. She looked up. There was no one in sight.

"Maid of France," the voice continued. "Daughter of God, stay close to God and go to church often."

Everything was silent again. Joan felt bewildered. She stood up quickly, her eyes scanning the countryside. She was completely alone.

"Who are you?" she asked shakily. "Where are you? I can't see you."

No one answered.

3

THE SAINTS

"Joan! You're daydreaming again! Try to keep your mind on your work," her mother chided. "Just look at how you've mended this stocking.... Everything you've done today has to be done over!"

"I'm sorry, Mother. But can I go out now?"

Her mother shook her head. "All right. But will you promise to do better tomorrow?"

"Yes," Joan answered. "I promise!"

Out in the fields the voice called again. It was evening and the bells of the nearby church were chiming the Angelus. Again the voice was telling her to be good, to love God and to go to church often. Again Joan heard only the voice. She saw nothing. Yet this time she wasn't afraid. She instinctively felt the goodness of the messenger. *He must come from God*, she thought.

"But who are you?" she asked aloud. Again there was no answer.

The next day, however, the mysterious

And then Joan saw the angel with her own eyes.

visitor identified himself. "I am the archangel Michael," he told Joan. And then she saw him with her own eyes. A light glowed around him and his face was the kindest Joan had ever seen. Other angels were with him, and they all looked so peaceful and happy! But soon enough the vision faded into nothingness. Joan was alone again. She wept because she couldn't go with the angels. Falling to her knees, she began to pray, "Oh God, I promise that from now on I'll be completely yours. I'll do everything you tell me to. Everything."

The days stretched into weeks and months until somehow three long years had skipped by. The girl who had first listened with terror to strange heavenly voices was no longer a child. Joan was now sixteen years old—lively, mature, sensitive and amazingly practical. She never learned to read or write, but in sewing and weaving Joan was second to none.

The long walks in the meadows continued. Mrs. d'Arc didn't mind as long as Joan got her chores done and did them well.

Joan will make a fine wife for some lucky young man, her mother thought. *And then someday I'll be a grandmother,* she added with a smile. Little did Mrs. d'Arc know how Joan would break this expected pattern of life.

The voices came more often now. Joan eagerly looked forward to her conversations with her new friends. Saint Michael no longer came alone or just with angels. Now he brought with him two other great saints, Saint Catherine and Saint Margaret. Together the three saints taught Joan how to live a holy life. Above all, they began to prepare her for the special mission God was going to give her.

Over time it began to make sense to Joan why these saints should be appearing to her. First there was the archangel Michael, the best loved of all the patron saints of France. Joan knew that the simple peasant folk had faith that God's angel would drive out France's enemies and make their land free and whole again. She had often heard people—beginning with her mother—pray that God would send Saint Michael to protect and defend them.

In those days, families would gather around a blazing fire in the evening. Parents would tell their children stories from the

Bible and the lives of the saints. How well Joan knew the story of Saint Michael! It had begun ages before God had even created the earth. Lucifer was a beautiful angel who had been very close to God. But then he chose to rebel against his Creator. The other angels chose sides between God and Lucifer, and a great battle followed. Saint Michael led the angels who had remained faithful to God. Michael's army won and drove Lucifer's rebels into a fiery exile where they would never be close to God again.

Even the Dauphin, France's uncrowned king, was devoted to the archangel Michael. Since God always hears our prayers, it made sense to Joan that Michael would come to rescue the struggling country that was so devoted to him.

The second voice Joan heard was soft and feminine. It was that of Saint Catherine of Alexandria. Joan knew Saint Catherine's story. Catherine, born in the year 313, had been a wealthy and beautiful daughter of an Egyptian king. A holy hermit taught her about Jesus and the Christian faith. The young girl listened eagerly, savoring every word. She believed and became a Christian.

At that time the powerful Roman Empire

with its emperor Maximinus had taken over Egypt. The emperor's rule was absolute. So when Maximinus demanded that all Christians go to temples and worship the Roman gods, the people knew that to refuse meant death.

Catherine was ushered into the temple. Her turn came to toss a few grains of incense to the Roman gods. She refused. God was the one true God, and Catherine knew it was wrong to worship anyone else. Two guards roughly dragged her before the emperor. Maximinus treated her kindly at first.

"Just offer a few grains of incense to our gods," he said, "and then you can go home again."

"I can't!" Catherine insisted.

"I'll put you in prison," the emperor sternly warned.

"Then do as you must," Catherine answered.

Fear gripped her as the guards grasped her by the arms and pushed her toward the door.

"You still have time to change your mind," Maximinus urged.

"I can't adore anyone but the true God," she firmly replied. "Take me to the prison!"

The wife of Maximinus overheard the

story of young Catherine. She felt inspired to visit her in prison. The empress went not just once, but again and again. The dark-eyed, innocent young girl spoke with such love and conviction that the empress couldn't help but believe in Jesus. She was soon baptized.

Maximinus was furious. He ordered his soldiers to kill his wife. Catherine knew that the same fate awaited her. But she stood firm. She was mercilessly tortured and then beheaded. But the incident didn't end in defeat. Her life and story brought strength and courage to many other Christians. Now, a thousand years later, Saint Catherine was bringing her message to a girl in France.

The third voice belonged to another saint from early Christianity. The young daughter of a wealthy, non-Christian judge, Margaret of Antioch was beautiful, clever, and loved by all.

Then one day a new maid came into the family home. She began talking to Margaret about Jesus. Margaret had everything that the world could give. But it wasn't enough. She was searching for something more. And she found it in the God of the Christians.

When her father discovered that Margaret had been baptized a Christian, a member of the very group he hated and persecuted, he refused to recognize her as his daughter. She suddenly found herself living in poverty and having to work hard, a condition she had never been in before. But Margaret was willing to give up all she had for God. And soon enough this would include giving up her very life. Persecutors of the Church killed her because she refused to renounce her love for God.

Now Saint Margaret had come to help a girl called to save a nation. Her quiet inspiration would give Joan strength.

These three great saints spoke to Joan. After they had taught her how to live a holy life, they began communicating another much more frightening message....

4

Too Incredible!

"Daughter of God," the voices urged Joan, "you must leave this village and travel farther into France. You must lead the Dauphin to Rheims so that he may be rightfully crowned."

"But I'm just a girl," Joan pleaded in desperation. "How can I do as you say? I can't even ride a horse, let alone fight all the soldiers between here and Rheims!" The idea seemed totally ridiculous. Besides, Joan didn't *want* to listen to the messages anymore. She didn't *want* to leave her family. She didn't even know how she could.

But Joan did know one thing. She knew that she wanted to obey God more than anything else. And God was telling her to lead the people of France to freedom—absurd as it may have seemed to her or to anyone else.

The voices did not give up. For many months they persisted with their unbelievable message. Joan became more and more frustrated. She increased her prayers each day, begging God to tell her what to do. At last Saint Michael outlined a definite plan for her.

"Daughter of God, go to Robert de Baudricourt in the town of Vaucouleurs," the angel told her. "He will give you soldiers who will take you to the Dauphin. God will help you. God will be with you."

Joan didn't protest. She was finally beginning to understand. She knew that she wasn't capable of doing any of these things—*but God was.* All she had to do was say yes and trust him. Then God could work through her to accomplish whatever he wished. If he wanted to, he could even use her to save the battered country of France.

Joan renewed her promise, knowing full well that her mission would be difficult. "Lord," she prayed, "my life is totally yours. Use me as you wish."

What would my father say if he knew about all this? she wondered. *I've never told him about the voices. If he knew that I'm planning to leave home and raise an army to try to save France, he'd lock me in a room and never let me out!*

Joan worried that she might not be able to leave without making her parents suspicious. But God again stepped in.

Durand Laxart, Joan's cousin by marriage, lived not far from Vaucouleurs. Just at that point he asked Joan to come and spend some time with his family. Of course, her parents agreed.

Durand was a poor farmer but a good man. He was the first person Joan told about her voices and mission. She asked him to take her to Robert de Baudricourt, the captain of the Dauphin's armies in Vaucouleurs.

Durand was speechless. *This is all too incredible,* he mused, *my young cousin hearing voices of angels and saints who tell her to lead an army that will save France!*

To stand before de Baudricourt—a man powerful enough to determine the fate of poor peasants like themselves—would call for real bravery. Durand knew how ridiculous they would look. He really wanted no part in the whole affair. But for some reason, he couldn't say no.

The day for the planned visit arrived. Joan nervously straightened her faded red dress as she turned to her cousin. "Are we ready?"

Durand silently nodded.

The two walked to Vaucouleurs and climbed the hill to de Baudricourt's fortress. The gates to the Great Hall were wide open, and people were freely coming and going. Joan whispered a prayer, "God, I don't know how to do this. Please make me brave and give me the right words." Then she confidently walked up to the powerful leader.

"My Lord has sent me," she began calmly, "to tell you to send word to the Dauphin that he should be prepared, but not yet go out to fight his enemies. My Lord will send him help before Lent ends. This kingdom does not belong to the Dauphin, but my Lord wishes the Dauphin to become king and to care for the nation. The Dauphin will be made king in spite of his enemies, and I myself will lead him to be anointed and crowned."

De Baudricourt stared at Joan in amazement. Silence fell over the room. After a few long seconds the nobleman thundered, "Who is this Lord you speak of, and what right has he to give orders to the king?"

Joan answered simply, "He is the King of Heaven."

The onlookers burst into laughter. Joan burned with embarrassment. She wanted to turn and run as far away as she could. Instead she stood there, silently begging God for strength.

After his own hearty laugh, de Baudricourt turned to Durand. "Take this little girl and her big stories home. Tell her father not to spare the rod with her. A good spanking should teach her some sense!"

All in the room burst into a new round of laughter as Joan and Durand made their exit.

De Baudricourt didn't believe her. But what hurt Joan more was the fact that he was refusing God's help. *I won't give up, God,* she prayed as she silently trudged along beside her cousin. *You can use me to answer the prayers of your faithful people.*

Robert de Baudricourt was an educated and capable military man. It never occurred to him that France might actually lose the long drawn-out war. Yet from the day that he sent Joan away, the odds against him began to mount. Soon the English and Burgundians combined forces and smashed through the last French stronghold, the Meuse Valley, which protected Vaucouleurs. Next the enemy overran Vaucouleurs itself. De Baudricourt ended up paying the invaders huge sums of money, to prevent them from destroying the town. But Joan's village of Domrémy wasn't so fortunate. Soldiers raided it and burned many homes.

English troops continued to land on French soil, and by October 1428 they held Orleans under siege. If this great city fell, all of France would be lost.

Several months flew by. Joan's voices were rallying her to new action. Her cousins, the Laxarts, were expecting their first child, and they asked Joan to come and help. God was giving her another chance to visit Robert de Baudricourt.

5

A Second Try

Durand accompanied Joan back to the now English-infested Vaucouleurs.

Once again they found de Baudricourt in the Great Hall of his castle, looking totally self-confident. But this time his attitude was only a sham. The English were conquering France. The situation was hopeless. And he knew it.

Robert de Baudricourt wasn't laughing now. He was desperate. All human means had failed him. There was no one left to turn to but God. Strangely, as Joan stepped into the room that day, the military captain felt a stirring of hope in his heart.

De Baudricourt looked into Joan's clear, pleading eyes. This time he saw that she sincerely believed her message came from God. This time he was ready to listen.

"God has often let me know that I must go to the Dauphin," Joan announced. "This is his will. The Dauphin is the true king of France. God will give me an army so that I may recapture Orleans and lead the Dauphin to be crowned at Rheims."

De Baudricourt was taken aback. The idea that Joan's proposal was "God's will" made him uneasy.

"Come again another day," he told her. "I need time to think this over."

Joan calmly nodded and turned to leave. Her cousin Durand followed her out. The two found a kind couple, Catherine and Henri Royer, who offered to let them stay at their house. There Joan helped with sewing and spinning, filling all her extra moments with prayer. Once, while the Royers were speaking sadly about the problems caused by France's Queen, Joan looked up from her spinning. "Haven't you ever heard," she asked innocently, "of the old prophecy that France, lost because of a woman's sin, will be saved by a maid from Lorraine?"

Catherine almost gasped in surprise. Of course the couple had heard of the prophecy. Everyone in France knew about it. But as Joan spoke, the prediction seemed suddenly very close to home. From that moment on Catherine and Henri believed in Joan and her heavenly mission.

Almost eight months had passed since Joan's first visit to de Baudricourt. Her impatience to set out to see the Dauphin was growing day by day. Now, even after more conversations, the French captain was still delaying providing her with an escort to the Dauphin. Two of de Baudricourt's soldiers finally decided to take matters into their own hands.

Twenty-eight-year-old Jean de Metz set out to speak with Joan himself. He appeared at the Royer home one day, requesting to see her. When she came in, de Metz asked almost teasingly, "What are you doing here? I thought you must have long gone to the aid of the king. Or must we all turn English?"

Joan's dark eyes flashed. "I've come to this town to ask Robert de Baudricourt to lead me to the king," she answered solemnly. "But he doesn't pay any attention to me. Yet, before mid-Lent I must be with the Dauphin, even if I have to wear my legs down to the knees from walking there. No one on earth, no king or duke or any other person can restore France. Only I can do it," she said with amazing humility. "Still I would much rather be at home helping my mother with her spinning. I'm not cut out for a life of fighting. But I must go. I must accept whatever my Lord wants me to do."

"Who is your Lord?" de Metz asked in amazement.

"He is God."

Right then and there de Metz took Joan's hands between his own and swore on his soldier's honor that he would lead her to the Dauphin. He was soon joined by his military comrade, thirty-six-year-old Bertrand de Poulengy, an old friend of Joan's family. De Poulengy too made an oath to safely escort her to the Dauphin.

But de Baudricourt would not let them leave for several long, torturous weeks. Joan's impatience rose to fever pitch.

"When should we start?" the two soldiers asked her.

"Better today than tomorrow and better tomorrow than later," she replied. Joan couldn't understand why de Baudricourt was stalling. Her voices were demanding *immediate* action.

On February 12, 1429, Joan again went to de Baudricourt. "You've already waited too long," she scolded. "Today the Dauphin suffered a great loss near Orleans, and he will suffer many more unless you send me to him."

A few days later news reached Vaucouleurs that the Dauphin had indeed lost a major battle—just as Joan had said.

De Baudricourt was struck with terror. He quickly sent a message to the Dauphin in Chinon. The Dauphin replied by sending back a messenger ordering Joan to come to him.

Joan would travel with six escorts. De Metz and de Poulengy would be joined by their respective serving men, as well as by Colet de Vienne, the Dauphin's messenger, and Richard, the Dauphin's archer.

Joan decided that it would be best if she dressed like a man. De Metz and de Poulengy agreed. In this way, looking like a court page, the seventeen-year-old wouldn't call any attention to herself and would be safer among the men. Joan cut her hair and slipped on the riding breeches, black cloak, woolen cap and soft leather boots the villagers had made for her. De Baudricourt attached to her belt the special lightweight sword he had had designed. The soldiers had also bought her a spirited steed to ride. The *curé* came to give the group his blessing.

Joan knelt on the ground, while the men stood by their horses. All was now ready for the journey to Chinon.

Joan took a deep breath as she mounted. "Help me to do this Lord," she whispered as the horse bucked and snorted in protest. The men climbed into their saddles. In a moment the seven were galloping down the road.

"Go! Go! God be with you!" de Baudricourt called after them. "And let come what may!"

6
THE DAUPHIN

Soon the riders could no longer see Vaucouleurs behind them. Gone also was the region of the Meuse Valley. They had lost sight of all that was familiar to Joan. Never again would she see the peaceful little village of Domrémy.

Frigid winter winds clawed at them as the group sped along the frozen dirt road toward Chinon—about 375 miles ahead. Even de Metz and de Poulengy, so used to the outdoors, suffered the penetrating cold. They couldn't light a fire. It might give them away to the bandits and enemy soldiers prowling the area.

Joan's uncovered face felt chapped and numb, but she never complained. What really bothered her was that she could no longer assist at daily Mass.

They watched her, those men who had vowed to bring her safely to the Dauphin. They watched her carefully. Their admiration and reverence for her soon grew into awe.

"There's nothing bad in her," de Metz whispered to de Poulengy. "I tell you, she's a saint, a real saint."

They rode on and on. A few times they managed to arrive at a church in time to attend Mass. Eleven days passed. Joan's muscles ached; her whole body was sore and stiff. She tried to remember Jesus' sufferings and death. *This isn't too bad,* she prayed, *when I think of all you went through for me.*

At last they entered Fierbois, near Chinon, where the Dauphin resided. Joan dictated a letter that one of the men took to the Dauphin, asking if their party could see him. Permission was granted. The next morning, the dusty, unkempt group advanced to Chinon. Joan was jubilant.

The Dauphin kept them waiting until that evening before admitting them to an audience. Never had a country girl seen anything like it—a splendid palace, blinding in its beauty. Brilliant torchlight illuminated the Great Hall. Although Joan, still dressed in her boy's attire, stood out in stark contrast against the backdrop of glittering gowns of ladies-in-waiting, her bearing and expression radiated something strangely noble.

"My dear," a snobbish woman whispered, turning to a friend, "look at the way she's dressed. What a disgrace to enter the palace like that!"

"Just a poor peasant pretending to be important," another hissed.

A hush fell over the Great Hall. The assembled knights and nobles glared in mute silence. All eyes were riveted on Joan. She paid no attention.

A gentleman of the court stepped forward to lead Joan up to the front of the room. Although she had never met the Dauphin, Charles VII, Joan knew that he was not the man smiling down at her from the throne. She turned and scanned the crowd. Her heart was pounding. *Help me, Lord,* she prayed. *Only you can save France. Make up for what I lack. I want to do your will.* Slowly she walked toward the real Dauphin, who had mingled in with the other nobles in an attempt to trick her. A murmur ran through the crowd as Joan knelt before him. How long she had waited for this moment!

"May God give you a happy life, sweet King!" she exclaimed.

"I am not the king," Charles replied. Pointing to one of the nobles he said, "He is, not I."

"In God's name it is you and you alone who are the king," Joan calmly responded.

"And who are you?" Charles answered back.

"Gentle Dauphin, I am Joan the Maid. God has sent me to help you and your kingdom. You will be anointed and crowned in the city of Rheims. This will make you a leader answerable only to the King of Heaven, who is the one true king of France."

The Dauphin stared at Joan in disbelief.

"I would like to speak with you alone," he half whispered.

7

"My Good Duke"

They talked for a good while—just the Dauphin and Joan. Simply and honestly she told him everything. She described her heavenly voices and the mission to save France, which God had entrusted to her.

"Even though it seems impossible, I am the only one who can do it," Joan concluded firmly. "God has chosen me to save our country."

"How am I supposed to believe this...this fantastic story?" the Dauphin sputtered. "I need proof—some sign that it's all true."

"On All Saints Day of last year, you went into the chapel of your castle alone and prayed for a long time," Joan found herself saying. Then she went on to repeat to him exactly what he had prayed.

The Dauphin gazed at her thoughtfully. What she had said was true. Every word of it. No human being could have known this unless God had revealed it. Charles believed the dark-eyed peasant girl standing before him. The day would come when he would betray her, and leave her to a terrible and unjust fate. But his belief from that day on would never waver. It would be conquered only by his cowardice.

The board of examiners eyed Joan intently. Powerful church leaders—including priests belonging to the Benedictine, Carmelite and Dominican Orders—were called in to question her. Charles thought that others needed to declare that Joan was being truthful in order for her to gain the support she needed. The sessions dragged on for three weeks. Joan's nerves were razor sharp. All she could think about was the battered city of Orleans barely surviving the English siege while these men hammered her with pointless questions.

"What kind of language do your voices speak?" an examiner with a thick accent asked.

"A better one than yours," Joan answered dryly.

"Do you believe in God?" he challenged.

"Yes. More than you do."

"God cannot wish us to trust in you," broke in another questioner, "unless he sends us a sign."

Joan slapped her hand on the table. "Just lead me to Orleans," she cried, "and I'll show you the signs for which I was sent!"

Around and around the questions went. Yet never once did they confuse her. And never once did she contradict herself. When the monks and theologians began thumbing through their yellowed books to find new objections, Joan simply observed, "Our Lord has more books than you. He has books that you've never read."

Following much discussion and further deliberations, the court of examiners issued their report. It read, in part: "After examining her life, her conduct and her intentions, we find in her all things virtuous: humble, pure, prayerful, honest and simple."

Joan was now one step closer to Orleans.

Although God was behind the mission to save France, he had chosen to work through human beings. So Joan needed the support of the nobles.

It wasn't easy for these powerful men to allow an untrained peasant girl to lead them. But little by little some of them began to abandon their pride and learn to trust.

"Just lead me to Orleans, and I'll show you the signs for which I've been sent!"

The Duke of Alençon was one of these. A young and handsome soldier, he held the respect of the men he commanded. The Dauphin introduced him to Joan.

"I've heard of you," the duke said as he shook her hand, "and I believe in you," he added simply.

"Good, because all the nobles must band together for our cause," Joan assured him. They were friends from that day forward, and the duke's loyalty never faltered. Joan spent a few days with him and his wife before they set out.

"I promise you," she told his wife, "I will see that he returns safely after the war is won."

Joan never spoke of Alençon by name; from then on she would always refer to him as "my good duke."

8

SWORD AND BANNER

The town of Tours was famous for its manufacture of suits of armor. Joan stayed there in a small house as preparations were being made to recapture Orleans. Pierre and Jean, two of her brothers, had also come to Tours.

Since she was going into battle, Joan needed a suit of armor specially molded to fit her. When she first tried on the shiny metal outfit, she felt as though she had been pinned into a coffin. *I'll do this only for you, God,* she prayed. A leather holster was then fastened to her waist. But when they tried to slip a sword into it, she resisted. "No," she said strangely, "Not this one.... I know of a better one."

As soon as the bulky armor had been removed, Joan sat down to dictate a letter to the priests in the town of Fierbois, where she had assisted at Mass on her way to Chinon.

"Behind the main altar," she directed as a soldier hurriedly scribbled her words, "you'll find a sword with five crosses engraved on it. Please uncover it and send it to me. It's the sword I must wear into battle."

The message was sent. The priests searched behind the altar. And the sword was discovered, just as Joan had described it. When the caked dirt had been chipped away and the powdery rust removed, the shining sword was found to be in perfect condition. The good fathers wrapped the treasure in velvet and sent it on to Tours.

Joan next commanded that a banner of white linen ending in two points and fringed with silk be made. Since it would be difficult for an army to recognize and follow its leader once the visor of his helmet was lowered (everyone dressed in armor would look the same) the banner that the leader or someone close to him carried was important.

Saint Catherine and Saint Margaret described to Joan what her banner should look like. She entrusted the task of making it to a famous Scottish painter living in Tours. The words "Jesus" and "Mary" stretched across the top of the banner in letters of gold. On one side, Jesus, represented as the King of Heaven, sat with his right hand raised in blessing, and holding in his left hand the globe of the earth. To his right and left the angels Michael and Gabriel knelt in adoration as each presented Jesus with a *fleur-de-lis*, a French symbol resembling a lily. The reverse side showed a blue background on which a white dove was flying. On a banner flowing from its mouth were printed the words, "In the name of the King of Heaven." The entire background was dotted with *fleurs-de-lis*.

Joan also had a pennant made, a kind of small pointed flag. It pictured the scene of the annunciation, with the angel Gabriel handing Mary a *fleur-de-lis*, which is also a symbol of chastity.

There was only one last preparation to make before setting out for Orleans. On Tuesday, April 26, 1429, Joan went to confession. She had all her men do the same. The next morning the whole camp assisted at Mass and received Holy Communion.

Now God's soldier and her army were ready for battle....

By this time Orleans was in real trouble. The English were continuing their attacks and the city was like an open, festering wound. Its food supply was nearly gone.

There were casualties on all sides and no areas to care for the wounded and dying. Despair held the city in its frightening grip.

By Wednesday, April 27, Joan and her army were on the march toward Orleans. Priests and friars led the way chanting the hymn, "Come Holy Spirit." Joan rode behind them in her shining armor, accompanied by a squire bearing her banner, and Captain Etienne de Vignolles, better known as La Hire. Next came the main body of the greatest soldiers in all of France—about 3,000 archers and men-at-arms, headed by the country's military officers, and a large group of nobles, knights and captains. Surrounded by the protective troops, a long line of supplies advanced toward the starving city—nearly 600 wagons of food and ammunition, hundreds of heads of cattle, and herds of sheep and swine.

As news of the army's approach spread, cries of hope echoed through the streets of Orleans.

"Joan the Maid is coming to save us!"

"The Maid of Lorraine is finally on the way!"

9

ON THE MARCH

As they rode on, Joan cringed to hear La Hire repeatedly cursing and using indecent language. The captain was known as an excellent soldier. But he was equally known for his bad mouth.

Finally Joan couldn't stand it any longer. She maneuvered her steed alongside La Hire's. "Captain, if you want to be my friend," she challenged, "you must stop that cursing. In fact, I restrict you to all oaths but one—the one I use myself—'In God's name.'"

La Hire growled beneath his breath, but he agreed. And, incredible though it may seem, he never swore again!

La Hire's heart was as big as his massive body. He became Joan's self-appointed guardian. After all, the brave girl was young enough to be his granddaughter. The captain had the most ingenious way of taking care of all the extra details which Joan's limited knowledge of military tactics wouldn't even permit her to imagine. Of course, he never let her know this.

One of La Hire's greatest gifts was his ability to ease a tense or even desperate situation. As they rode closer to Orleans, he saw how nervous and frightened Joan looked. The captain leaned over in his saddle. "Your voices said we'd win, didn't they?" he encouragingly growled.

"Yes," she agreed meekly.

"So, then we will!" he thundered. "Let's go!"

Later on, as they rode side by side into battle, La Hire would bellow the famous prayer that always made Joan smile: "Lord, I pray you do for La Hire what he would do for you, if you were La Hire and La Hire were God!"

They marched on, hugging the banks of the Loire River. The French military planners had thought it best to keep the river between them and the besieged city of Orleans. Joan's voices, however, had told her to meet the English head on.

"You've tricked me!" Joan protested when she realized that the men, acting on orders sent from Orleans by Commander Dunois, had led her to the wrong side of the river. Upset and angry, she refused to listen to their further plans.

Twenty-six-year-old Dunois, a cousin of

the Dauphin and the leader of the garrison that was doggedly holding Orleans, was intelligent and courageous, bearing almost no resemblance to his royal relative. He sincerely believed that Joan had been sent by God.

As the French army settled for the night on the eastern outskirts of Orleans, Dunois himself rowed across the river to welcome the Maid, although the rain was falling in torrents and the Loire was dangerously swollen. He greeted Joan warmly. "I'm grateful for your arrival," he confided with a smile.

"Is it your doing that we're on this side of the river?" Joan shot back.

Dunois looked down at the muddy ground. "We've done what we thought was wisest," he said quietly.

"In God's name," she retorted, "our Lord's advice is better and wiser than yours!"

The commander didn't try to press the issue. He knew that by human standards he was right. But this was no longer a human struggle. It was supernatural. It was divine. Dunois suddenly came face to face with the shocking reality that a greater Commander than he was leading the French army.

"I'm sorry," he mumbled in confusion. "From now on we'll do as you say."

10

ORLEANS

Dunois had carefully planned how to transport the supplies and food which Joan and her army had brought for his starving city. He had just enough barges ready to carry the provisions across the river and into Orleans. Now his strategy was being ruined—not by the English—but by the wind. The heavy barges were as useless as paper boats because the wind was blowing wildly in the wrong direction.

Joan stood gazing out at the choppy water. "Don't worry," she said confidently. "The wind will change, and the English will not move against us."

Almost instantaneously the wind shifted direction. The French military leaders stood watching, as if in a trance. Dunois shook them back to reality with his shout. "Forward!"

The English scouts watched as the caravan of barges carrying lifesaving supplies neared Orleans. But they did nothing to interfere! If Joan the Maid were from God, who could stop her? If she were a witch, the devil himself was on her side. Whatever their reasoning, the frightened English stayed away. Even in this, the will of God was fulfilled.

At eight o'clock the next night, anticipation ran high. The people of Orleans awaited the answer to their desperate prayers.

A watchman's cry suddenly shattered the silence. "Here they come! The Maid is approaching the Burgundian Gate!"

Thousands of torches lit the way as Joan and Dunois, followed by the French troops, trotted through the gate. Crowds streamed from everywhere, from hallways and doorways, from alleys and cellars. Men, women and children—the entire town—surged into the dusty streets to welcome the girl whom God had sent to save them. Shouts of joy rang through the chill air. In the English camp men shivered in fear. The witch of Lorraine had arrived!

Riding on her white steed, Joan looked glorious. Her armor reflected the blazing torchlight. Her banner and pennant danced in the wind. Joan the Maid, the virgin of the prophecy, had come at last!

The parade marched through the city to the Church of the Holy Cross. Joan entered the church and knelt to converse with her Lord.

"My God, I'm afraid," she whispered. "But I mustn't let anyone know.... Give me the courage to do your will!"

Joan emerged from the church with renewed confidence and strength. Only prayer could make her strong enough, brave enough and persevering enough to carry out God's commands. With prayer she would fight. And with prayer she would win.

11

VICTORY

Joan, fully armored, sat atop her white stallion on the narrow bridge just beyond the city walls. The strongest of the English forts lay directly in front of her.

"In the name of God," she shouted, "surrender and I will grant you your lives!"

"You miserable cow-girl," a rough English voice called back, "if we catch you we'll burn you alive!"

Joan reined in her horse toward Orleans. Her heart was heavy. She had failed in her second attempt to give the English a chance to retreat. Now they would have to fight.

Four days slid by. Joan was waiting, not at all patiently, for Dunois to return from the town of Blois with more troops. The English knew that Dunois was away. It would have been the most logical time for them to attack. But they didn't move—not even an inch. What if the French peasant girl was really a witch?

Joan walked through the streets of Orleans. She stopped to greet each of the

French citizens she passed with a friendly word and a warm smile. These acts of kindness worked greater miracles than any medicine could have for the frightened and suffering people.

"Wait!" one old woman breathlessly called, as she hurried up to Joan. "Touch this rosary for me!"

Joan laughed heartily. She knew she had no more power than anyone else. All she did came from God. "Touch it yourself," she teased. "Your touch is as good as mine."

Meanwhile, Dunois, accompanied by 500 reinforcements, was nearing Orleans. When word of this reached Joan, she and her party rode out to meet them, escorting them safely back to the city—in full view of the English.

Later, as Joan was eating her meal of a few hard bread crusts dipped in water, Dunois came to interrupt her.

"Sir John Fastolf, the great English general, is approaching the city with supplies and men," the commander reported. "He despises you, Joan."

"Let me know when he gets here," she replied excitedly, "or I swear I'll have your head!"

"Don't worry," replied Dunois. "I promise to let you know."

But once again the French officers acted on their own, this time planning an attack without Joan's knowledge. It was her voices that came to the rescue.

In early afternoon, Joan retired to her room to rest. She hadn't been there long when suddenly she bounded from bed. "My voices have told me to go against the English! But they didn't say whether to attack them in their forts or to go deal with Fastolf, who is coming with supplies," she shouted wildly to her hostess and armor bearer. "My arms! Bring me my arms and my horse! Why didn't you tell me? The blood of our people is staining the ground!"

In a matter of moments she was armored and mounted. Her banner and staff were dropped to her from the second floor window. Sparks flew from the cobblestones as her stallion charged down the street. Joan didn't know where to go, and yet the horse was galloping toward the Burgundian Gate. She halted there as a badly wounded soldier was being carried in.

"Who is he?" Joan asked weakly, her face deathly pale.

"A Frenchman," the men answered.

"I can never see French blood without my hair standing on edge!" was her only reply.

She spurred her horse on. Her voices now told her where to go. The fields of Saint-Loup came into view. Fifteen hundred Frenchmen were trying desperately to storm a key English fort, but the English were winning hands down.

Hoisting her pennant into the air, Joan charged forward to rally her army. She led the Frenchmen in an immediate, all-out assault. With new strength the men rushed ahead and took the fort.

The accounts are not exact, but all agree that a great number of English soldiers were killed, many taken prisoner, and the fort burned to the ground. Only two French lives were lost. Joan's presence had transformed a desperate situation into victory. But she felt no joy. So many men had lost their lives before they had been able to confess their sins. She wept for them.

"Thank God for this victory," she told her army. "If you don't, I'll leave you and no longer help."

In every church throughout the countryside the people recited special prayers and sang hymns of praise. Bells rang joyously for hours while the English listened with shattered courage.

The French had won a victory.

But the greatest battle was yet to come.

12

LAST CHANCE...

"They must have one more chance," Joan thought aloud.

"Who?" someone asked.

"The English, of course."

She had offered them the chance to retreat twice before. But she had to try again.

Joan spent all of Ascension Day, Thursday, May 5, in prayer. She went to Mass and felt God's love burning within her as she received Jesus in the Holy Eucharist. She again ordered that all her soldiers confess their sins.

Meanwhile, the officials of the French army were back to their planning. And again their council didn't include Joan. Dunois grew nervous at the thought of how angry she'd be when she found out!

It wasn't that the military leaders were purposely ignoring her. Unconsciously they had labeled her as a saint—not a soldier. They considered her a kind of good luck charm, whose very presence brought victory. But when it came to military strategies, what could she possibly know?

The leaders agreed upon a new battle plan. Only then did they approach Joan. Dunois acted as their spokesman.

"Tell me what you've decided," she begged, trying to remain calm.

"Joan," Dunois began kindly, "don't be upset. We can't tell you everything at once. Tomorrow we'll attack the fort of Saint-Laurent, but if the English along the south of the river should go to assist it, we'll cross the river and attack the forts there."

Joan quickly grasped the situation. Dunois believed in her totally. So did La Hire. The common soldiers and the entire city of Orleans were willing to follow her with blind and total devotion. But the highest military officials were not.

Joan felt hurt and confused. She was angry with the men who had made decisions without her. The victory of Saint-Loup had come from God, not from their plans. They had lost before. They were winning now. Wasn't that proof enough that her voices told the truth? But what could she do? Soon enough she forced a smile and agreed to the plan.

That evening Joan dictated a new message to the English. One of the priests took it down for her.

"You men of England have no right to be here in the kingdom of France," the letter read. "The King of Heaven commands you through me, Joan the Maid, to leave your forts and return to your own country. If you will not, I will make a noise such as will never be forgotten. I write to you for the third and last time." She signed the note, "Jesus, Mary, Joan the Maid," and then added a request that the English release her herald, who had been captured.

The letter was fastened to the end of an arrow and shot from the bridge into the enemy camp.

The English laughed and jeered as they read it. "Go back to your fields, witch!" they shouted, calling Joan every ugly name they could think of. They did, however, release her herald.

Tears streamed down her face. The battle would take place the next day. Because they refused to listen to God's message, many would suffer and die.

Friday dawned clear and brisk. Joan awoke as the first rays of light cut the darkness. She hurriedly dressed, went to Mass and received Communion.

The French officers had chosen this day to execute their battle plan. But the citizen soldiers of Orleans, hot and impatient, had a plan of their own. They thronged in a massive body to the Burgundian Gate. Captain de Gaucourt had shut, locked and barred it. He, loyal to his orders, refused to budge. The tension was mounting dangerously when someone had the good sense to send for Joan. She and faithful La Hire jumped into the saddle and rushed to the scene.

"You're wicked not to open the gate!" Joan shouted to de Gaucourt. "Whether you like it or not, these men will go out and defend themselves!"

Joan was for them. To the men this meant God was on their side. They stubbornly pressed on.

De Gaucourt was white with fear. If he opened the gate, the army's leaders might have him killed. If he refused to open it, the pack of agitated men might rip him to shreds. He decided to throw in his lot with Joan. As the gate swung open, de Gaucourt shouted, "Forward! I'll be your captain!"

The armed mob swarmed across the countryside like angry bees. It finally came face to face with the English, who were holding out in an Augustinian monastery that shielded their major stronghold—the fort of Les Tourelles. The French citizen soldiers proved to be no match for the English, who fought brilliantly. It nearly turned into a massacre....

Joan was not with the patriotic citizens who attacked the enemy. She and La Hire had remained behind to summon the regular French forces. Now they were storming to the rescue—a vast throng of fresh soldiers with the Maid and La Hire in the lead.

"All right you miserable...," La Hire's words stuck in his throat as he met Joan's icy stare. "Er...a...in God's name," he added quickly, "advance!"

The day ended in another great victory for France.

13

THE BATTLE

Saturday, May 7, 1429. "There will be no fighting today," commanded the French officers. They were at it again; trusting their own plans—not God's—to lead them. These proud men just couldn't get used to accepting orders from a young peasant girl, even if she had been sent by heaven to help them!

But the people never lost their faith in God, or in Joan his servant. Some of the citizens of Orleans approached her. "We've consulted together," they confided, "and we've come to beg you to fulfill the mission given you by God and the Dauphin."

"In God's name, that I will do!" she promised. Leaping onto her steed she cried, "Let those who love me follow me!"

They did love her. And they would follow! Every able-bodied Frenchman ran for his horse. The soldiers also rallied. Ignoring the decision of their leaders, they joined the excited civilians.

Clouds of dust enveloped the town as Joan, Dunois, La Hire and the men bolted through the gate. "God wills it!" came the cry of patriotic voices. "God wills it!"

The Battle of Orleans had begun.

Near the end of a bridge on the south of the Loire stood the powerful fort of Les Tourelles. Six hundred English soldiers perched inside it, their bows drawn taut, their arrows aimed and ready.

The French worked their way up to the enemy fort, but each time they attempted to hoist their ladders and scale the walls, English arrows cut them down. The battle dragged on until noon. When the Angelus bell rang out, the fighting ceased for a few minutes. Joan prayed the Angelus with her soldiers. Soon she was back in the thick of the fighting. At one point, pushing her fears aside, she seized a ladder, threw it against the fort, and bravely began mounting the rungs.

I'm their leader, she told herself. *I must lead by example.*

Suddenly she heard a whirring sound. An arrow sped by her face, sinking itself deep into her shoulder. She plunged from the ladder. The English began to cheer. They had finally downed the witch!

An arrow sped by her face,
sinking itself into her shoulder.

Only then did Joan show that she was frightened. She began to cry softly as the French carried her to safety.

"You'll pay for this!" La Hire bellowed at the English. "In God's name, you'll pay!"

One of the Frenchmen gently eased off the top portion of Joan's armor. The arrow had penetrated about six inches into the flesh. Joan herself bravely pulled it out, after having been encouraged by a vision of her saints.

With the arrow gone, the wound bled dangerously. A soldier dressed it with olive oil and lard in an effort to stop the flow. Then Joan made her confession. "Rest, now, Joan," her chaplain begged, "at least until the bleeding stops."

"Only until then," she answered weakly.

As she lay there, she heard whisperings among the men.

"The sun will soon set," one murmured. "The English aren't backing down. How much longer can we fight?"

"What can we do without the Maid?"

"We should retreat," a third voice nervously broke in. "Where's Dunois? He must call a retreat!"

Joan sat up. "Dunois!" she cried. "Dunois! Wait! We must not retreat! Help me with my armor," she ordered a soldier. "Dress me up.... I'm going to fight!"

Dunois was bending over her now. "Joan, I think we should sound the retreat," he said wearily.

"No, no!" she pleaded, clutching his arm for support. "Fight just a little longer and in God's name I promise you we'll take the fort! Now have the men rest and take something to eat. Bring me my banner!"

Joan winced as she got to her feet. Entrusting the banner to one of the soldiers, she turned toward the men gathered around her. "When you see my banner touch the wall of the fort, attack!" she commanded. "The victory will be yours!"

The banner bearer galloped off toward the English fort. The others watched as Joan moved a short distance away. There, by the bloodstained battlefield, Joan of Arc fell to her knees in prayer. The scene gave her troops new courage. *Help us, my Jesus,* she pleaded. *Fulfill your will. Saint Michael, fight for France!*

Returning to the waiting captains after about a quarter of an hour, Joan mounted her horse. "Courage!" she cried, spurring the steed forward.

Joan's shout and the sight of her white

banner leading the way rallied the men. Behind her thundered the army of France—soldiers and townspeople alike—surging across the field like a dark, menacing wave.

Up ahead they could see it now, the Maid's banner fluttering against the side of the English fort! A mysterious burst of energy rushed into the Frenchmen. They flung up ladders on all sides of the fort and scaled them with ease.

The English stood frozen at their posts. Hadn't they killed the witch? Hadn't they seen her fall to the ground, stabbed and bloodied by one of their own arrows? And yet she was back—riding and commanding her troops as if nothing had happened!

By the time the English took hold of themselves, it was too late. The French were everywhere.

The wooden drawbridge was now the Englishmen's only escape. About forty of them began pushing and fighting their way across it toward safety. They didn't realize that as darkness fell, a number of French soldiers had slipped beneath the bridge and set its supporting framework on fire. The French, warned by the shouts of their comrades, now abandoned the English on the bridge. The flames had already eaten halfway through the beams when some of the heavily armored English officers threw their full weight onto the bridge. Joan recognized the English commander as one of these. "Glasdale!" she shouted, "surrender your soul to the King of Heaven! You called me a witch, but I have great pity for your soul and the souls of your men!"

But Joan pleaded in vain. Glasdale had no intention of giving up.

The weakened bridge could take no more. Cracking loudly, it suddenly collapsed, hurling the English through the flames into the angry Loire below.

A horrified Joan watched as the men sank out of sight, dragged down by the weight of their armor. She wept.... And she pardoned them.

Within the fort hand-to-hand fighting continued. But not for long. Fresh troops poured in from Orleans and took the surviving English captive.

Soon the battle scene grew quiet. Only the joyful pealing of church bells broke the silence as the victorious French army made its way back to Orleans. Torches lit their way and women and children sang hymns in the streets. Joan smiled down from her saddle. God had won his victory!

On the following day, Sunday, the English abandoned their remaining forts and left Orleans—never to return.

14

CORONATION DAY

Joan was frowning.

Dunois shot her a look from his saddle. "What is it?" he asked as the group rode along toward Tours. "After such success, you should be smiling!"

"My voices say the task is not complete," she answered thoughtfully. "The Dauphin must be crowned at Rheims."

"There are a lot of Englishmen between here and Rheims," Dunois observed skeptically.

"But my voices insist," Joan replied.

The Dauphin, too, was traveling to Tours, but from a different direction. Joan arrived there first and rode a short way out of town to meet him. She removed her boyish cap and bowed low before him. The Dauphin didn't say a word. He too removed his hat— a rare mark of respect on his part—and lifted her bowed head. Several witnesses say that in his joy he then gently kissed Joan on the forehead. She asked for an audience, and her request was quickly granted. But it would take several meetings before Joan could persuade Charles to go to Rheims.

At one of these, Joan knelt before him. "Noble Dauphin," she declared, "don't speak or debate too much. Come quickly to Rheims to be rightfully crowned."

"Do your voices tell you to say this?" one of the noblemen present asked.

"Yes," Joan simply replied, "and they speak urgently about it. When I'm angry because the words of God I speak are not believed or acted upon, I go apart and pray to him and tell him that no one has faith in what I say. Then Jesus tells me, 'Go forward, child of God; go and I will help you.' I am overwhelmed with joy and wish I could listen to that voice forever."

"I will go to Rheims," the Dauphin promised, "but you, Joan, must precede me with your armies to clear away the remaining English strongholds."

Joan smiled and nodded. Her voices had instructed her to do exactly this. She and her armies went on to win victories at Jargeau, Meung, Beaugency and Patay. The road to Rheims was now clear.

It was July 17, 1429, approximately six months since Joan had left her town of Domrémy. The scent of freshly cut flowers filled the great cathedral of Saint-Remy. The morning sun pouring through the stained glass windows bathed the waiting congregation in brilliant hues. Lilies adorning the thick-walled basilica contrasted with the dazzling costumes of the French nobility.

"Greetings, my good Duke," Joan whispered to Alençon as he filed into place. Somewhere in the huge crowd were also Joan's father, her two brothers and her cousin, Durand Laxart. In fact, in a few short hours she would be in her weeping father's arms, begging his forgiveness for all the pain she had caused him. The blessing he would give her would complete Joan's happiness that day.

Charles, the Dauphin, was kneeling now before Regnault of Chartres, the Archbishop of Rheims. The five-hour ceremony was about to climax. One of the priests stepped forward bearing the crystal cruet with its sacred oil. The archbishop's voice rang clearly through the massive church: "With this holy oil, I anoint you king, in the name of the Father, and of the Son and of the Holy Spirit. Amen."

A solemn hush fell over the crowd. Then three times the archbishop exclaimed "Long live the King!" The bishops, priests and people took up the triumphant shout, "Long live the King! Long live the King!" as trumpet blasts shook the great cathedral.

Throughout the entire ceremony Joan had stood by Charles' side in her polished silver armor. Now she was one of the first to do him homage. She couldn't hold back her tears as she fell to her knees before him. "Noble King," she said with emotion, "the will of God has now been done. He is the one who commanded me to raise the siege of Orleans and bring you here to Rheims to be anointed and crowned, to show all that you truly are the king of France."

The day of joy and consolation over, Joan realized that the main part of her mission had been accomplished. What would God now have her do? She wasn't sure, but she trusted that whatever it was, he would be there with her.

15

A Broken Heart

Joan, Alençon and their men spent the summer months fighting and winning minor battles with the English up and down France. Joan urged the king to storm Paris, then under English-Burgundian control, assuring him he would win an easy victory. But Charles brushed aside her advice and decided to negotiate for the city instead. (When he later allowed Joan to lead an attack on Paris, a retreat was called against her wishes, thwarting the French siege.)

The Duke of Alençon, bored with the inactivity of the French court, asked for and received permission to return home. He was relieved. Plenty of English had intruded into his territory. It was time to push them out.

"My good Duke, can't I come and rid you of the English?" asked Joan.

"Will you?" the duke responded eagerly.

"No," the king replied for her. "She's staying here at court!"

Tears filled her eyes as Joan murmured, "My good Duke, you've always been my dearest friend. You believed when no one else did. You believed without need of proof or signs. I can never thank you except through prayers.... We won't meet again on this earth. There's just one more thing I must tell you. You won't like it at all." She hesitated.

Alençon stared at her intently.

"I'm going to be captured and betrayed and..."

"Yes?" he anxiously prodded.

"And imprisoned," she said quietly. "My voices have told me so. It's God's will." Joan turned toward the window to hide her tears. "You will try to save me, but you will fail. Yet, I will rejoice that you tried."

"No!" Alençon choked. "No!" And he wept without shame.

But Alençon could do nothing more. The next day he left for home.

"Farewell, my good Duke," Joan called. Her eyes followed the noble until he and his stallion faded into a tiny speck on the horizon.

La Hire, Joan's other faithful friend and supporter, left soon afterward to fight the English in Normandy. Next Dunois was called away. These were bitter moments for the soldiers and lonely times for Joan. It pained them all to leave the liberation of France incomplete.

"Well, what do you expect," La Hire had grumbled, "when your king's a coward!"

Joan found life in the palace dull and unhappy. She could never get used to the sophisticated and haughty manners. Since she didn't have many friends, she kept to herself. Joan spent the long and lonesome hours speaking to God in prayer.

At one point, in a gesture of gratitude, Charles conferred the title of nobility upon her and her family. Joan sometimes heard the king's voice echo in her imagination, "I raise you and all your family to the rank of nobility for the countless and manifest signs of God's grace which have been bestowed on us because of your intervention...."

But another inner voice clamored to be heard. *Words, just words,* it told her. *You'll soon see how much he loves you.*

16

CAPTURED!

"The English still hold many French cities," Joan constantly reminded the king. "We must *do* something!"

Meanwhile, her voices continued to speak to her. "Joan," they told her, "you will be captured before the feast of Saint John. But do not be afraid. God will help you."

It was already the beginning of May. The feast of Saint John the Baptist would be celebrated on June 24....

Joan couldn't stand by watching the king repeatedly refuse to help his people. After much prodding, she finally talked him into letting her ride on a few minor campaigns.

Margny was not big enough to be a city. In fact it could best be described as a hamlet. It was a Burgundian outpost. The Bur-gundians, of course, were Frenchmen who had sided with the English. They were powerful, ruthless and very well organized. Joan's army had just about liberated the town when a large enemy troop appeared from nowhere, closing in on them from all sides.

Joan's 500 men, never having expected this, panicked. They struggled, frantically fighting their way toward the drawbridge that led back into the town.

"We're lost!" someone called to Joan. "Back to the town! It's our only chance."

"No, no!" Joan cried. Had these men no faith in what her voices were telling her? "Play your part and we'll beat them!" she shouted. "Forward and they are ours!"

One of the few soldiers who had remained with her grabbed the reins of Joan's horse and tried to lead her to safety. They could still make it.... Then—it couldn't be—the drawbridge started to rise. The only way into the city was sealed off!

Joan and a few faithful men were left outside. The Burgundians closed in on them with lightning speed. The Maid of Orleans was cruelly knocked from her horse and taken prisoner. It was 6 p.m. on May 23, 1430. Never again would Joan taste freedom.

The Duke of Burgundy was gloating over his good fortune. The news of Joan's capture would increase his fame—not to mention the contents of his purse! Ah, yes, the English would give anything to get their hands on the witch. They wanted nothing more than to make her pay for the humiliations she had caused them in battle. But if this were true of the English, what about the French? Wouldn't they pay a much greater ransom for their precious heroine? "This is too wonderful to be true," snickered the duke.

The news of Joan's capture alarmed all of France. A well-loved archbishop sent an urgent message to King Charles: "To ransom and recover this girl, you must spare neither means nor money. If you do, you will be disgraced forever for monstrous ingratitude."

Then came letters from the Duke of Burgundy offering Charles every chance to buy back France's best-loved citizen. Charles felt uneasy each time a new message arrived. But he never sent a reply. Neither did he ever lift a finger to save Joan. He had silenced his conscience, the voice of God.

La Hire, Dunois and Alençon thundered

away at the king: "You must save her! She'll die if you don't buy her freedom. The English will surely kill her!"

But it was no use. Charles refused to make the decision himself. He allowed himself to be influenced by his friends, most of whom were jealous of Joan. "Forget her," they insisted. "She was always such a nuisance, telling us what to do. It will be good to be rid of her!"

Joan was more afraid than she had ever been in her life. The nine-foot-thick walls of her tower prison seemed to close in on her. Her imagination played ugly tricks, filling her mind with images of torture and pain.

Discouragement and depression struggled to overcome her as she waited day after day for her king to ransom her. Her one hope was prayer. Prayer made Joan realize that she was never alone. Jesus was there with her. No matter what they did to her, he could never be kept away.

17

FAILED ESCAPE

"What are you going to do with me?" Joan asked weakly.

"Ah," the Duke of Burgundy chuckled. "A very good question. I'm going to sell you to the highest bidder, of course." He laughed a long and vulgar laugh. "Back to your room!"

The guards roughly led Joan away and locked her in her quarters. Standing watch at the door, they took turns ridiculing her.

"You're not afraid, are you, Maid?"

"Talk to your voices. They'll keep you company!"

"Why do you hate me?" Joan cried.

"Because you're a witch!" answered a mocking voice, followed by howls of laughter.

"Leave her alone!" sounded a shrill woman's voice. "You're not to talk to her again, do you understand?"

A key clicked in the lock and the door swung open. The Duchess of Burgundy entered Joan's cell, her face flushed in anger.

"Leave her alone!"

Joan was sobbing quietly. "Don't be afraid," the Duchess said gently, sitting down beside her.

Joan continued to pray and hope in her lonely exile. As the weeks ticked by, summer cooled into autumn. It was painfully obvious that her king had forgotten her. But she refused to dwell on the thought. "Oh, God, be my strength," she begged. "I can't do this without you."

Joan smiled when the Duchess walked in that day. But she immediately realized something was wrong when the older woman didn't smile back.

"What is it?"

"I'm sorry," the Duchess whispered as she bent to embrace her. "I'm so sorry," she sobbed loudly. "You will be sold to the English...."

Joan felt dizzy with fear. Her voices had been telling her the same thing. *What will the English do to me?* It was too horrible to imagine.

Later, she heard the guards laughing as they discussed a planned attack on a nearby

French town. "No one will survive, not even the women and children," they boasted.

Joan couldn't just sit there and let it happen. She *had* to escape. But there was only one way out....

She scanned the area beneath the tower. From her vantage point, seventy feet up, even the castle moat looked tiny. The guards behind her were busy talking. They would never suspect what she was about to do. Joan quietly moved to the tower's outer ledge. Taking a deep breath, she hurled herself into the air.

The faces bending over her were hazy and blurred. Her entire body throbbed with pain. But Joan was conscious enough to recognize angry shouts as she was carried into the fortress.

Back under guard in her cell, she wept. "Why didn't you help me, Lord? I don't understand."

Saint Catherine finally replied. "You were trying to escape on your own, Joan. You didn't stop to listen to the voice of God. That town will be saved, but it is not

God's will that you should be the one to save it. You are to stay here and remain faithful to God."

"I'm so sorry, my Lord" Joan sobbed. "I want to do only what you want, not what seems better to me. Help me. Please help me to trust you."

18
THE TRIAL

A gray castle overlooking the English-held town of Rouen was to be Joan's new prison. The echo of men's heavy footsteps drowned out the sound of her own as they led her down the halls to her place of confinement.

Joan studied the large room. It would be her home from December 23, 1430 until February 21, 1431. Dank and musty, it was thick with cobwebs and layers of dust. The guards threw her onto the straw bed. "You'll have some trouble breaking out of these, Maid," one promised as they clamped heavy metal chains to her wrists and ankles and secured them tightly to the bed.

Christmas came and went. Lying helpless in her prison, Joan's only joy was to think that she was suffering everything for Jesus—who had been born in an equally damp and drafty stable.

Her trial was set for February 21. Carefully chosen royal and Church officials were to decide whether Joan was a heretic. Pierre

Cauchon, Bishop of Beauvais, would preside. The ambitious Cauchon, a man unfaithful to his God, hoped through English influence to become archbishop of the great city of Rouen. He hated Joan, whose army had defeated the city where the English and Burgundians had made him bishop.

Cauchon knew that if he could find Joan guilty of heresy, the English would grant him even more power and pay him greater respect. After all, they hated her too. Cauchon had only to condemn Joan to death. And that he would willingly do. To make sure everything went as planned, he would go so far as to personally choose all the priests, judges and doctors who were to conduct the trial. If any of these happened to speak in her favor, the evil bishop would use his power to silence them or have them punished.

February 21 arrived. The courtroom was filled. The judges stared as a haggard-looking girl dressed in boy's clothing walked to the front of the room. Joan's hair had grown. Falling straight, it reached almost to her shoulders. Her usually lively brown eyes appeared bloodshot and tired.

They could have killed her quietly and buried her in an unmarked grave, but they didn't. The English wanted Joan discredited as a heretic and a witch. The taste of revenge was as bitter in their mouths as the memory of so many French victories was fresh in their minds. A woman had been responsible for those victories. Now she would pay!

"Admit that your voices aren't real!"

"Tell the world you're lying!"

"Your power comes from the devil!"

"Are you a witch?"

Accusations and questions were flung at Joan in dizzying speeds. Words much too large for her to understand were used. She knew that the judges were trying to twist the truth and confuse her. And through it all she was left without the help of a lawyer.

"Do you hear your voices here?" someone questioned.

"Yes, I hear them."

"And what are they telling you?"

"They tell me to answer you fearlessly!"

No matter how confusing and misleading the questions were, Joan responded as best she could, telling only the truth. She amazed her interrogators with the clarity and depth of her answers. Cauchon soon realized that making Joan appear evil was not going to be easy.

The trial dragged on for almost five months. During that time her captors assembled between 200 to 300 persons to question and accuse her. The English got more frustrated as each day passed. And their treatment of Joan grew harsher. They even molded an iron cage and wheeled it down the stone corridors to her prison room.

"We'll put you in there," a guard threatened, "if you don't admit that you're a witch."

By this time Joan was thin and sickly, but she hadn't lost her spirit.

"At least it will protect me from people like you!" she snapped back.

As her suffering worsened, the voices sent by God comforted and encouraged her. God did not abandon her.

19

THE VERDICT

Six public and nine private trial sessions later, Bishop Cauchon and the English Earl of Warwick came to visit Joan.

"Just retract the statements about your visions," the bishop began with false kindness. "Admit that your voices aren't true, and we'll set you free. Do you realize what that means? You will be free to go back to your town and family and everything you love."

Joan stared at him.

"But if you don't," he added harshly, "you'll be condemned to death. And do you know how a witch dies?" Not waiting for an answer, he bellowed, "By fire!"

"Fire?" Joan repeated as the color drained from her cheeks. "Fire?" she murmured again. Of course she had known that a condemned witch was burned at the stake, but she had never actually imagined herself in those flames.

"You're going to make a public retraction now, aren't you Joan?" Cauchon pressed.

She never heard him.

Sleepless nights, physical torture and lack of food had all taken their toll. How tired she was...how very tired. Her face was rigid and white. Although her lips were still, she was conversing with her voices. Even if a war had been thundering in that room, Joan wouldn't have heard it.

"Of course you're going to retract," the bishop confidently mumbled, as he rose and strode arrogantly from the room.

A crowd had gathered in the cool, damp cemetery of Saint-Ouen on the morning of Thursday, May 24, 1431.

Joan was brought there in a cart. The judges asked her for a statement denying that her voices came from God. Now she heard. Now she understood.

"No!" she shouted with renewed energy. Turning to Bishop Cauchon, she cried, "God *has* truly sent me and my voices *are* from him."

But during the course of this new "trial," Joan was cleverly tricked into signing two documents. These falsely declared that she was now denying what she had testified about her heavenly voices. She was promised that if she signed, she would be taken out of English custody and handed over to Church authorities. If she didn't sign, she would surely be burned at the stake as a witch.

Not knowing how to read, Joan believed what she had been told. After tracing her name on the declarations, she joyfully exclaimed, "Now lead me to your prison, men of the Church!"

But it had all been a cruel trick.

"Take her back to her cell!" Cauchon ordered the English guards.

Bishop Cauchon again interrogated Joan in prison. He led her into a conversation about her voices. During the discussion Joan protested that she had never intended to deny her voices. She had only signed the documents because she wanted to be tried by the Church, not by the English, and because of her great fear of fire. Without ever having the second document she had signed read to her, Cauchon declared her a relapsed heretic (someone who had fallen back into heresy). He then got the other judges to agree that she should be handed over to the English authorities. They would decide her fate.

It was certain to be death...by fire.

20

A Mother's Grief,
a Father's Pain

Jacques d'Arc nervously paced the floor in the gray, pre-dawn light. He felt terribly helpless and alone.

"Jacques," his wife's voice whispered softly. "Come to bed now. You've been up all night. It's almost daybreak."

"Already?" he asked fearfully. "It's morning already?"

"Yes, of course. But...but why do you ask, Jacques?"

How could he tell her? For so long now, he had worried about this moment. He had known it would come, but how he had prayed that it never would! Jacques sat on a stool with his head almost touching his knees. "Isabelle," he said slowly, "there's something we must talk about."

Mrs. d'Arc drew close to her husband. "I know you're worried about Joan," she answered as she hugged his tired shoulders. "All we can do is trust God—trust that her voices will bring her home again. She can't possibly be condemned to death, Jacques. She's just a child...and she's done nothing wrong. Nothing. We must believe that."

The hours ticked by. Jacques sat motionless as his wife prepared a breakfast that no one was going to eat.

The sun rose higher, but the farm work was not begun. "Begin your work," his wife encouraged. "Take your mind off Joan. Today we must do as all the other days."

But this was *not* like any other day that Jacques d'Arc had ever lived through or would ever live through. This Wednesday, May 30, 1431, would burn a wound into his soul that not even a thousand lifetimes could heal.

It was 8 a.m. The position of the sun told him so. Now he would tell his wife. He had to.

"Isabelle," he said, holding her tightly, "This will hurt you very much. But the time has come to tell you...." His voice trailed off in a whisper. "Joan has been condemned to death.... She's dying...now...this morning."

"No! My God, no!" the poor woman wailed. She began to tremble uncontrollably. "But...how...how is she dying?" she groaned.

"Don't make me answer that now," her husband choked.

"How is she dying, Jacques? You must tell me!"

"By…fire."

"No, God, not that…not fire!" Isabelle shrieked. "Oh, Jesus," she sobbed, falling to her knees, "please take away the pain! Take away the fear! She was always so afraid of fire!"

21

To Heaven

A crowd of over 10,000 was anxiously milling about the square. Compassionate faces, hardened faces, indifferent faces, sneering faces, laughing faces—all were fixed on Joan. She stood before them on a wooden platform. Her male clothing was gone now. In its place a plain white dress fell softly to her ankles.

Bishop Cauchon rose. The crowd fell silent as he read the sentence. "....We pronounce you in the name of the law to be excommunicated and a heretic...."

Joan's face paled with the realization that the terrible fire would soon be lit. Panic raced through her body. She scanned the crowd. Where were her friends, her parents, anyone who might stand up for her?

Earlier that morning she had gone to confession and received Holy Communion. Just now, after again declaring her innocence and the reality of her voices, she had spent a tearful hour in prayer. She had forgiven those responsible for her death. She had requested that Masses be offered for her. Nothing more remained to be done.... But her terror remained.

As they led her off the platform, Joan turned to the sympathetic priests who accompanied her. "Won't they give me a cross?" she pleaded. An English soldier could no longer hold back his pity. He broke a branch in two, hurriedly tied the pieces into a rough cross, and handed it to Joan. Meanwhile, one of the priests ran to a nearby church to get a crucifix. He returned with a processional cross just as Joan was stepping out of the cart that was transporting her to the place of execution. Joan fell to her knees and tightly clutched and kissed the crucifix.

Next she was led up the steps to another platform that had been prepared. There she was securely chained to a concrete stake encircled by heaps of wood. *Jesus, I can only die like this with you,* she prayed in her heart.

They were coming now—the men with the lighted torches. The burning tips were touched to the brittle straw packed between the wood. Loud crackling was heard as tongues of fire lapped at the piles of logs. In a few moments curls of smoke began to rise from the flaming mass. The flames leapt higher. Joan's white dress was ablaze now.

Joan needed the crucifix more than ever, although her bound hands could no longer grasp it.

"Get back, Fathers, or you'll be burned!" she shouted to the priests who were trying to comfort her. "But please...please hold the crucifix before me until I die!"

One of them hoisted the processional cross into the air. Higher and higher the image of Jesus rose through smoke and flames until it met Joan's eyes.

She could be heard softly moaning and praying. "Saint Michael," she begged, "you who promised that out of these flames you would lead me into heaven, help me to be strong!"

Soon the flames were so high and the smoke so thick that Joan could no longer be seen. Only her voice could be heard above the crackling of the fire. "Jesus! Jesus!" she called over and over again.

Yes, Jesus was with her. She was no longer afraid. She would soon be freed of every suffering. She would soon be led to heaven.

"Jesus! Jesus!"

The bystanders, even the English, were sobbing now.

Eternal minutes passed. Finally one last, high-pitched cry emerged from the blaze, "J-e-s-u-s!"

A shocked silence followed.

Someone in the crowd wailed, "We've burned a saint!"

22

RESTORED HONOR

The English believed that they could conquer France once Joan was out of the way. They did enjoy a few more successful battles after her death. But then the Duke of Burgundy had a change of loyalty and transferred his massive armies to the side of the French. With this added military power, the French drove the English completely out of France. Another of Joan's predictions had come true.

Meanwhile, Joan's story had spread throughout France. The people considered her a martyr, a saint and a symbol of their united country.

The climate was one of unrest. Resentment against King Charles—the coward who had done nothing to save Joan—ran high among French nobles and peasants alike.

Charles could no longer ignore the terrible feelings of guilt that burdened his conscience. Neither could he ignore the clamor of those demanding that Joan's name be cleared. He finally decided to act.

And so on November 17, 1455, in the Cathedral of Notre Dame in Paris, Joan's trial was reopened. The appointed papal officials filed solemnly into the nave of the church. A crowd of people poured in behind them. Among these, an aging woman, wrapped in a homespun shawl, walked quietly to the front. With Isabelle d'Arc were her two sons, Pierre and Jean. The three were now the only surviving members of Joan's family.

The Church, in which Joan had never lost trust, sought the truth about Joan's life and mission for eight long months. Witnesses were called in to give testimony concerning her life in Domrémy, on the battlefield, in prison and during the trial. Then the investigation was moved to Rouen, the city of her death, where new witnesses were heard. All evidence pointed conclusively to the fact that Joan's first trial had been unfair.

The verdict of the commission was handed in to the Archbishop of Rheims, who publicly proclaimed it:

"We, from our seats of judgment and thinking only of God, say and decree that the trial and condemnation of Joan the Maid was tainted with fraud, malice and gross error of fact and law; and that this trial and condemnation, together with the retraction and the execution and all their consequences, were and are null and void and are to be disregarded."

Even in those days before newspapers, radio and television, the news spread quickly throughout France. With great rejoicing, every city and town held processions in Joan's honor.

But the Lord himself restored Joan's honor in a way she would have never dreamed of.... On May 9, 1920, nearly five hundred years after her death, the Roman Catholic Church officially canonized Joan of Arc. More than being God's soldier, Joan was now one of his saints!

PRAYER

Saint Joan, your life was really one of love, faith and courage. It took so much of all three to do everything that God asked of you!

God will probably never ask me to lead an army to free my country. And I'll never be visited by angels or saints. But God does want me to love and obey him before anyone or anything else, just as you did.

Help me to know God's will, Saint Joan, and to do it well. Help me never to avoid doing what I know is right and pleasing to God because I'm afraid of what others will say or think of me.

Give me the courage to follow Jesus wherever he leads. Pray for me, Saint Joan. Amen.

GLOSSARY

1. **Angelus**—a prayer that honors the mystery of Jesus' Incarnation (the fact that Jesus is both true God and true man). The prayer consists of three verses alternated with three Hail Marys. According to custom, it is prayed three times a day: at 6:00 a.m., at noon and at 6:00 p.m.

2. **Archangel**—one of the chief angels.

3. **Behead**—to put a person to death by cutting off his or her head.

4. **Besieged**—surrounded by an enemy army.

5. **Canonize**—the act by which the Pope declares, after much research and the required proof of miracles, that a deceased person is a saint and may be honored by the whole Church.

6. **Chastity**—the virtue by which we keep ourselves pure in mind, heart and body.

7. **Conscience**—our inner sense of right and wrong that tells us if something is good and should be followed or if it is evil and should be avoided.

8. **Curé**—a French term for a pastor of a parish.

9. **Excommunicated**—the word **excommunicate** means "to exclude from a community." When a person is excommunicated it means that for some very serious reason he or she is not allowed to receive the sacraments, especially the Holy Eucharist.

10. **Fraud**—something meant to hide the truth from others.

11. **God's will (or the will of God)**—what God desires us to do at each moment of our lives.

12. **Hamlet**—a small village.

13. **Heresy**—a denial of a truth of the Catholic faith. A person who promotes a heresy is called a **heretic.**

14. **Hermit**—a person who lives alone, devoting himself or herself to prayer.

15. **Humility**—the virtue by which we realize that everything good in us is a gift from God.

16. **Loot**—to steal valuable items, especially during a time of war.

17. **Malice**—the desire to harm others in some way.

18. **Martyr**—a person who dies for his or her faith.

19. **Nave**—the middle section of a church.

20. **Null and void**—not binding under law.

21. **Procession**—a religious event in which people walk together from one place to another to publicly honor God, the Blessed Virgin or the saints.

22. **Processional cross**—a cross or crucifix that is mounted on a pole and carried in procession during liturgical celebrations.

23. **Retraction**—the act of taking back or denying something one has said.

24. **Squire**—a knight's assistant.

Daughters of St. Paul

I We Pray I We Preach I We Praise I

Centering our lives on Jesus, Way, Truth & Life

Witnessing to the joy of living totally for Jesus

Sharing Jesus with people through various forms of media: books, music, video, & multimedia

If you would like more information on following Jesus and spreading His Gospel

as a Daughter of St. Paul…

contact:

Vocation Director
Daughters of St. Paul
50 Saint Pauls Avenue
Boston, MA 02130-3491
(617) 522-8911
e-mail: vocations@pauline.org
or visit www.pauline.org

BOOKS & MEDIA

The Daughters of St. Paul operate book and media centers at the following addresses. Visit, call or write the one nearest you today, or find us on the World Wide Web, www.pauline.org

CALIFORNIA
3908 Sepulveda Blvd., Culver City, CA 90230; 310-397-8676
5945 Balboa Ave., San Diego, CA 92111; 858-565-9181
46 Geary Street, San Francisco, CA 94108; 415-781-5180

FLORIDA
145 S.W. 107th Ave., Miami, FL 33174; 305-559-6715

HAWAII
1143 Bishop Street, Honolulu, HI 96813; 808-521-2731
Neighbor Islands call: 866-521-2731

ILLINOIS
172 N. Michigan Ave., Chicago, IL 60601; 312-346-4228

LOUISIANA
4403 Veterans Blvd., Metairie, LA 70006; 504-887-7631

MASSACHUSETTS
Rte. 1, 885 Providence Hwy., Dedham, MA 02026; 781-326-5385

MISSOURI
9804 Watson Rd., St. Louis, MO 63126; 314-965-3512

NEW JERSEY
561 U.S. Route 1, Wick Plaza, Edison, NJ 08817; 732-572-1200

NEW YORK
150 East 52nd Street, New York, NY 10022; 212-754-1110
78 Fort Place, Staten Island, NY 10301; 718-447-5071

PENNSYLVANIA
9171-A Roosevelt Blvd., Philadelphia, PA 19114; 215-676-9494

SOUTH CAROLINA
243 King Street, Charleston, SC 29401; 843-577-0175

TENNESSEE
4811 Poplar Ave., Memphis, TN 38117 901-761-2987

TEXAS
114 Main Plaza, San Antonio, TX 78205; 210-224-8101

VIRGINIA
1025 King Street, Alexandria, VA 22314; 703-549-3806

CANADA
3022 Dufferin Street, Toronto, Ontario, Canada M6B 3T5; 416-781-9131

¡También somos su fuente para libros, videos y música en español!